Instrumental Music Teaching

A definitive guide to teaching in schools

Marie McNally

π

Acknowledgements

I have several people to thank for the creation of this book. The first is my mum who stopped me giving up the clarinet at age 15 and, consequently, gave me the career I now have. Next is my dad who gave me the support, encouragement and advice to get it finished, as well as helping to finance the project. Also Sarah who managed to put up with my erratic postage and helped to proofread the final copy.

And last but by no means least, Lee made this all possible with the purchase of an IPAQ and lots of hugs!

First published in 2006 by Pi Publishing
112 Astwood Road, Worcester WR3 8GZ

Copyright © Marie McNally, 2006. All rights reserved

The right of Marie McNally to be identified as the author of this work has been asserted in accordance with the Copyright, Designs and Patents Act of 1988.

A catalogue record for this book is available from the British Library.

ISBN 0-9553013-0-0 (978-0-9553013-0-8)

Designed and produced by au.

Cover illustration: Mandy Martin

Printed in the UK by Cambrian Printers, Aberystwyth.

Contents

Foreword

Dr Donald Hunt OBE

Marie's considerable practical experiences in the wider world of music-making and administration gives great credibility to her views and recommendations in this admirable book, which should be on the shelf – and regularly consulted – of all those who take their teaching seriously. She writes in a delightful style which is easy to read and deceptive in one way only, that it disguises her scholarship.

The library of books on music does not include many devoted to the art of teaching, and certainly few that express in such succinct terms so many aspects of the essential requirements to a successful career in this work that Marie so aptly describes as an 'organic profession', to which I would like to add the word 'vocation'.

This is essential reading for those who are beginning their teaching careers, with many helpful hints regarding employment techniques, and also for those who are looking for new ways of improving their teaching standards and making their lessons more stimulating for their students and themselves.

Dr Donald Hunt is Principal of the Elgar School of Music.

Introduction

How to use this book

The pages of this book contain some factual information, a few bits of historical stuff, some of what is I hope, useful advice, and some teaching pointers.

If you would like to, then please read the book from start to finish. I would be most flattered to think that someone has done so and that they may even have taken something useful from it. However, the book is designed for you to dip into at any point that you need. Therefore skip the bits you don't need and try out all the ideas that you think are relevant.

Teaching should be an organic profession. To be an effective teacher you should aim to constantly update and revitalise your approach. That's not to say that the traditional methods aren't important – you just need to keep the way you use them fresh and alive.

By reading this book you have made a positive step to do exactly that. With a bit of imagination I hope that you will then find countless ways of ensuring that you become a successful and effective instrumental teacher both in and out of the school environment.

1

Training to Teach

Instrumental teachers have traditionally been qualified through their own performance and instrumental teaching credentials. However, more and more musicians are needing to become qualified in the classroom rather than the music practice room.

Changing attitudes

So what has brought about this change in attitude? In short, there is a lack of accepted qualifications for an instrumental teacher. To become qualified one must complete teacher training such as a PGCE or equivalent, which usually involves no instrumental teaching whatsoever.[1] Perversely, some of the major instrumental teaching qualifications, such as the Associated Board's CTABSRM, do not count when it comes to County Music Services. Consequently, more and more instrumental teachers are taking the long route to qualified teacher status. But there are some clear benefits.

Employability

The most important benefit to your career is your employability. When music services advertise for instrumental teachers they usually require that the teacher is 'qualified'. Therefore if you are new to instrumental teaching, or thinking about moving jobs, it is in your interest to get the full teacher training certificate.

Financial benefits

To become a qualified teacher means to gain qualified teacher pay. This is linked to how many years you have been in service and will increase in line with inflation in the same way that school teachers' salaries increase. You can also apply for threshold payments, which means that if you achieve certain teaching and planning standards you will receive a higher rate of pay again. (It should also be noted however that private schools and schools which have opted out of the state music service system still work on their own rates of pay, which may or may not take into account qualified status).

Planning

Planning is one of the major areas of development for a trainee teacher but it is not necessarily developed by instrumental teachers unless they complete teacher training. As an instrumental teacher it is easy to 'wing' each lesson, developing work for your students on a weekly basis. Many teachers have taught this way for generations and it can be extremely effective as each individual gets their own training plan specifically designed for their needs. However, it can also lead to complacency. Learning how to effectively plan lessons has the benefit of making sure your teaching is

[1] *There are courses such as the PGCE at the Royal Northern College of Music which combine one year's study of instrumental teaching with one year of PGCE training.*

focussed. It will also help you to find new ways of approaching the same basic technique, which in turn keeps your teaching fresh and motivating for both you and your pupils.

Observing other subjects
One of the things you do as a trainee teacher, which you would probably never do otherwise, is to observe teachers in subjects other than music. Watching how other teachers develop ways of working in the classroom can suggest new tactics, which you can adapt to your own teaching repertoire. For example, watching the way that a drama teacher manages an improvisatory warm-up may suggest ideas for how you may use improvisation to start your own lessons. It is amazing how ideas can be adapted and reworked to suit your own teaching.

National Curriculum
As a trainee classroom teacher, you will find yourself developing the ability to cross-reference with the National Curriculum. Cross-curriculum learning is a major deal in schools today and all subject teachers are expected to teach literacy and numeracy as well as PSCHE (Personal, Social Citizenship and Heath Education) within their normal schemes of work. Instrumental teaching naturally covers some areas of numeracy and literacy. Having an awareness of other areas such as citizenship, and personal skills, will help to support the child's work in classroom and give your instrumental teaching in school strength and credibility.

Practicalities – the course
The practicalities of completing the training year are not easy, especially if you are already an established teacher. A PGCE usually means taking a year to study – which also means a break in income. However, some LEAs and Music Services will help with some kind of sponsorship, and some courses such as the Open University run them part-time (although the final teaching practice must be full-time). You will also receive a bursary of around £9000 (all figures are correct at the time of writing) some of which you will receive at the start and the remainder at the end of your training. In a new initiative you will also receive a £2500 'golden hello' once you complete your three-term induction. And don't forget that, as I said earlier, once you are qualified you will be paid at a higher rate, as well as being able to start to apply for extra threshold payments.

The induction year
How do you cope with a three-term induction when you don't want to go into the classroom? This is actually not as big a problem as it might seem. More music services are working through ways of completing the induction year

Useful Websites
Visit **www.tda.gov.uk** or **www.canteach.gov.uk** for further information about teaching in the UK.

www.teachinginscotland.com for information about teaching in Scotland.

www.openuniversity.co.uk for information about the OU's flexible PGCE, which many instrumental teachers have found useful.

whilst the teacher is in a full-time instrumental post. The newly qualified teacher must be attached to a school and the Head teacher must be prepared to sponsor them through the year. All standards must, of course, be met as in the case of any newly qualified teacher.

At this point in your training you will be assessed against your own instrumental teaching performance and training will be more relevant. Your abilities in the music practice room with individual and group lessons will be recognised, and you will maintain contact with other NQTs (Newly Qualified Teachers) through the courses which you will be required to attend (and get paid for).

This contact brings another added benefit. To complete teacher training means that you have to liaise with other teachers. You feel like you belong somewhere, instead of like a hobo with no fixed abode. You may still be moving between schools but you will be attached to one particular school, where you will have contact and support with a subject mentor, a school co-ordinator and the Head.

As this year draws to a close you should find yourself a polished, revitalised and excellent all-round music teacher. Ideas will be fresh and teaching material exciting and motivating. When you consider the overall benefits available the difficulties involved seem worthwhile.

This chapter formed the basis of an article in 'Music Teacher', July 2005.

Further Information

The TTA (Teacher Training Agency) is now the TDA (Training and Development Agency for Schools). They are currently developing a new framework of professional standards for schools – hopefully this will include a more practical route for instrumental teachers. QCA are also working on a new modernisation of the KS3 curriculum.

2

What Makes a Great Teacher?

Understanding how to fulfil your role as a teacher and analyse your teaching methods determines how successful you are. Ours is a profession where refresher courses are not often attended, frequently due to a lack of financial support (although there are many useful courses available). Traditional teaching methods run the risk of becoming stale and uninteresting unless we regularly update our understanding of our own teaching styles, take careful note of how our pupils are progressing and develop constantly changing ways of keeping them inspired.

The chances are that when a pupil first comes through the door it is because they have already found a love for an instrument. Our first job is to ensure that we foster that love. We need to help them develop a keen sense of musicianship, a thorough understanding of the instrument, and sound technique as well as help them to tackle musical literacy, and have fun along the way!

Instrumental skill

To be a successful instrumental teacher you must first of all have a clear knowledge of your instrument. This sounds obvious but to communicate with your pupil you must be able to play, and to play well. Music needs to be heard and pupils need to have an idea of what they are trying to achieve, which is most successfully demonstrated by hearing it. Learning by example is far more instinctive than any explanation. Whilst recordings can be wonderful, there is no substitute for hearing your teacher play. Think back to your own experiences. For many musicians hearing their teacher play to them is a moment they don't forget. After all, how many chances do we get to hear private performances from talented musicians in the luxury of our own music lesson?

Teaching other instruments

Many teachers find themselves teaching instruments that they are less familiar with. There are many jokes about teachers being 'a page ahead in Tune a Day'. However, this is a very unsatisfactory way to teach! The teacher must ensure that they are not unwittingly passing on bad habits. I would strongly suggest that a few lessons with an expert are necessary.

Early in my career I was asked to teach sax and flute. As a clarinettist I had dabbled in both but never been taught correctly. I had a few lessons with reputable teachers to ensure I had a sound technique, and took my Grade 8 in both – it was fun doing it and I felt much more confident as a teacher.

However, I have inherited pupils from teachers who have unwittingly passed on all manner of technical difficulties, stemming from a lack of understanding of the instrument. In several cases they gave up disheartened when they realised how hard it was to change bad habits and couldn't find the subtlety of tone required for later grades (see chapter 16).

If you feel that you are unable to master the technique of a new instrument then it is important that you question whether you are really able to teach it.

Lines of communication

As an effective teacher you should be able to communicate your thoughts and intentions clearly at the level which your pupil understands.

Don't over simplify or over complicate things. Explain things clearly and succinctly, demonstrating musical points by playing, singing or clapping.

Positive language should be used at all times. Everyone needs to believe that they can succeed in order to do so. Try to find something positive to say in each sentence such as 'that bar was good – let's see if you can do it with this one'. Reinforcement of any small achievement will help to drive your pupil towards greater success.

Always show confidence – feelings are contagious and any hint of uncertainty on your part, any loss of patience or negative feelings will be passed on to the pupil. Their response will be to lose trust and faith in you and you will struggle to regain a positive relationship.

Simple people skills such as providing a welcoming smile when a pupil walks in can go a long way to gaining their trust and making them feel comfortable. If in their first moments with you a child is happy then they will spend many progressive lessons in your company.

However, if a child is unhappy in their music lessons there may be a lack of practice, no progress made and consequent feelings of inadequacy. A downward spiral of avoided lessons, forgotten music, chatting and fidgeting to delay playing as long as possible, may eventually lead to the child giving up.

Questioning: pupils

Questioning is an art which class teachers establish early in their career, but instrumental teachers do not always learn or assimilate into their teaching routine. The following will help to develop your questioning style:

- Remember that learning music is cumulative. Don't take something for granted without explanation – for example, why a new piece suddenly has three beats in a bar instead of two, or the meaning of a pause sign. You may just find that something which you think your pupil should understand, actually needs reinforcing several times.

• For each new piece of music, question what each direction means, ensuring that the pupil has a full understanding of why they are playing andante. Don't be tempted to give the answers too quickly – encourage them to work out an answer if they don't know straight away.

• Always ask if they understand what you are telling them – never assume that something has simply gone in with no trouble!

• Asking a pupil to teach you what they have just learnt is one of the best ways of checking their understanding and consolidating their learning.

• Encourage them to ask questions as you go along as this will stop them hiding any lack of knowledge. It will also help you to understand their individual learning pace and build a trusting and confident teacher-pupil relationship.

• In group lessons encourage your pupils to ask each other questions. Make sure that all in the group are equally involved and show an equal level of understanding. Your pupils may find that they are more comfortable asking each other questions rather than asking the teacher (because be careful if the group dynamics aren't right then they will struggle with the confidence to ask each other).

Questioning yourself

Whilst it is important to continually question your pupils to check understanding, it is also important to question your own methods. Try asking yourself the following questions:

• Am I teaching this piece in the most effective way possible?

• Is the pupil engaged and showing a full understanding of what I am trying to tell them?

• Are they achieving what I want them to achieve?

• Are they playing to their best ability? If not how can I raise the standards?

• What different methods can I use that will keep my pupil interested and my teaching fresh?

By continually questioning yourself in this way you will keep your own teaching focussed and maintain high standards.

Reading your audience

Be aware of blank faces, always a give away that they have lost you! Staring out into space, looking at their watch, chatting when they should be playing, all suggest a loss of concentration and you will need to find a way of re-engaging their attention.

Be prepared to have to find several different ways of explaining something – for example, compound time often needs a mix of discussion, maths and demonstration! Use analogies that they will understand, and are appropriate to the age group, and check again and again whether they have understood your meaning!

Repertoire

You should use a varied repertoire, supplementing teaching books with other short pieces in varying styles. Not all pieces will be to their taste but encourage them to explore as many new genres as possible. Indeed, you should also try new pieces which are more to their taste – you may find your own taste expanding too!

Practice skills

Make sure that you work beyond the lesson and teach your pupil the skills they need to practice alone. They will need to be shown, for example, how to break down difficult passages into much smaller more manageable sections in order to make their practice effective. This subject is discussed further in chapter 4.

Integrated learning

Integrated learning is an approach which allows your pupil to develop both technically on their instrument, and musically at the same time. It is about teaching laterally and encouraging your pupil to multi-task. Instead of focussing on a single area such as a new note, or a new rhythmic pattern, include a full understanding of how to use that note or rhythmic pattern in context. For example, how loud should the new note be played and what technical difficulties will they encounter going from and to the notes on either side? To teach a true understanding of our instrument is to also teach a full understanding of the music itself. You should encourage a fully expressive and communicative performance of even the most basic pieces. You must fully convey all aspects of rhythm, pitch and stylistic awareness through an awareness of the instruments capabilities.

Teaching music in this way will provide a thorough and sound musical education for the pupil, and will help to keep lessons musically satisfying for both pupil and teacher.

Teaching expressively

Be aware that it is not always necessary to learn a piece of music before adding expression. To simply 'note-bash' in this way is to play and practice soullessly. Your pupils may develop an excellent technique but without the creative freedom to express what they are playing.

Try to encourage even the very first notes to be beautiful, with a full and even tone. Don't accept cold passages when they could easily be played with a little imagination and flare. Talk about how the music makes your pupils feel and experiment with playing it in different ways to encourage them to make their own decisions about mood. Even when sight-reading you should insist on a degree of expression to ensure that they are developing an overall sense of freedom and confidence.

Vocal skills

Kodaly wrote that 'a child who plays before he sings may remain unmusical for a lifetime'. There is much to be said for adopting a little of his philosophy. The voice is the most natural of instruments. To sing is to allow free expression without the restrictions of playing an instrument. Children who learn with the Kodaly method of teaching generally have sound and confident vocal and musical awareness. Once this is established it can be successfully transplanted to instrumental learning.

Using the voice often in instrumental lessons can seem a little strange if you and your pupils are not used to it. However, singing part or all of a piece can help the pupil to focus on the music away from the restraints of playing an instrument. It helps them to understand the sounds which they want to make before they actually try and make them. By singing the music they will internalise it – it will become a part of their musical make-up and when they come to play it there will be a much more profound understanding and degree of expression.

For younger children, try adding words to simple melodies or rhythmic patterns. This is fun and helps them to gain a stronger understanding of rhythm as well as helping to develop their aural skills. Work out different patterns of words to express the mood – for example, would your song have to be about summer time and having fun or about the worst maths lesson in the world?!

Similarly, writing short stories or drawing pictures can help to gain an understanding of mood. Colours in particular have a powerful effect, for example, thinking about red when you play a piece con fuoco. As a useful exercise, instead of setting scales that week perhaps your pupils could draw a picture of what they think the music is about?

Improvising with the voice can help to develop a wonderful sense of musical freedom. If a pupil is reticent about singing, some question and answer phrases, perhaps over a popular or jazz piano riff, can work wonders. You need to be able to demonstrate and sing out with confidence to enable them to follow. Remember an amazing voice is not necessary – simply the confidence to enjoy singing fun phrases and to encourage the same from your pupils.

Teaching aurally

Learning a piece by ear can be hugely beneficial and indeed provides the basis of teaching philosophies such as the Suzuki method, where notation is not introduced until a basic understanding of the instrument and musical awareness is sound.

Why not set your pupil a task of learning a nursery rhyme by ear instead of practicing a unit from a book. This works for any standard of player; more advanced pupils should be able to learn it in several keys, perhaps even travelling around a cycle of fifths, or develop it as an improvisation.

Performing opportunities

Music exists to be heard and it is important for children to have opportunities to perform and 'show off' their new skills. Do not leave this just for exams. Find out about school concerts where your pupils may be able to have a solo or group slot. Organise a pupil concert in the school hall or a local church and create a sense of occasion. Providing this kind of platform will give your pupils the confidence to grow as musicians.

3

The Lesson Plan

Most teachers find that they have a vague lesson plan ready to go in their head, which they build on as each lesson progresses. However, it can be helpful to spend a little time working through how you will plan your lesson. It helps to keep your objectives clear and will give you a sense of confidence, control and focus.

Give yourself and your pupil a plan by working out a time-scale for the work you are doing. This may be working for an exam or learning a new piece over a half-term period. It helps to define what the pupil should have learnt in that time and allow them to focus their practice. You should build supporting work into this plan such as scales, sight-reading and aural skills.

If you involve your pupils in this planning session it will help them to take responsibility for their learning, and takes no more time than a five minute chat at the beginning of their first lesson of that session. They may well suggest objectives which surprise you – either suggesting work that you yourself would have suggested, or something completely different but equally beneficial. In both cases support their ideas, make your own suggestions and find a middle ground, which allows you to agree a plan of action. You should then have a brief assessment at the end of the period, which allows the pupil to see their progress.

If the pupil does not achieve their goals then you at least have a starting point to work out what wrong. Any lack of practice will show up, though it may also be that your own expectations were too high, don't rule this out, especially with a new pupil.

For this reason it is also useful to have a broader goal in mind; perhaps during one term the aim would be to learn pieces for an exam and in three terms to take the exam. You should also be ready for any changes such as a sudden improvement or unexpected difficulty which speeds or slows progress. The general rule is to be flexible. It is important that pupils feel success, however small, in order to continue to improve.

You should keep weekly notes, which allow you to see if you and your pupil are on target. However good your memory may be, teaching a large number of students means it is easy to forget small details. Keeping notes also has the added benefit of making end of year reports easy to write (see chapter 11). Make sure that you keep a record not only of the lessons each week, but of what you need to look at the following week, and what work should have been achieved in the meantime.

The 'three-part lesson'

The three-part lesson is something that 'trained' teachers (i.e. PGCE or similar) teachers are familiar with and other teachers often do instinctively. It simply involves having a beginning, a middle and an end to organise each lesson.

Openers

The opening moments of your lesson are a good time to reflect on the previous lesson and discuss how practice has gone since. You then need to tell the pupil what you hope they will achieve in the next half an hour. Explain why they are going to do each activity, and make sure they understand fully.

They will then need to warm-up fingers and instrument effectively and there are many ways of doing this. The most often used is probably scales – not least as it gets them 'out of the way'. But try to make sure that they are relevant to the pieces being worked on and not just unrelated exam scales. This should help to eliminate the amount of times you are asked 'why do we have to do scales Miss'!

However, don't get stuck in a trap of using only scales as a warm-up. Some simple long notes, often forgotten after the initial grades, can be an extremely effective warm-up for any standard of pupil. This allows the breath control to kick in, positive posture to be set, weight on the bow arm to be settled and tone to gain a full and positive sound. Use dynamics to practice control of intonation. (Of course this applies mainly to wind and string instruments).

Another good way of starting is by working with rhythm away from the instrument. This is the perfect opportunity to work on any difficult patterns in the pieces being learnt – for example, clap the rhythm of some sight-reading which deals with swing rhythm or compound time. Musical games are also a fun way of engaging your pupils attention. Some ideas can be found in chapter 13.

Main section

This is the section which most instrumental teachers find most satisfying as it is where you should work on the pieces being studied. Listen and correct them, play them together, discuss them, break them down, accompany them on piano or simply play them together to reinforce or correct any problem areas.

Don't feel that you need to hear everything that has been prepared. If you find that you spend some time working successfully through a single difficult point, but then run out of time to hear the other pieces, then they can keep working on them until next time. As long as you have a balance over a period of weeks and are able to ensure that they are making overall progress then you are doing a good job.

If you are starting a new piece don't be afraid to play it to them first. Hearing you perform will give them confidence as well as something to aspire to. However, don't let them rely on you to perform every new piece. Perhaps sometimes they could sight-read it or learn small parts of it first, to ensure that they are playing it correctly and will be able to continue to get it right after the lesson. After all, how many times have we heard 'I couldn't practice 'cos I forgot the tune Miss'!

Finish

At the end of the lesson is another good time for some musical games – a quick musical terms quiz or 'guess the rhythm' game are fun and can consolidate any learning from the main body of the lesson, for example, by continuing to use compound time. You also need to make time for the boring bits – make sure that you have included a summary of the lesson, reinforcing what they have learnt. They should have everything written in their notebooks, know when their next lesson / rehearsal is etc. Perhaps get them to do a summary themselves each week. They should leave full of positive ideas about how to achieve their weekly goals. Send them out of the lesson with a smile!

Coping when it all goes wrong!

This is much easier for instrumental teachers than classroom teachers as we have a wealth of material to draw from. In your armoury always have an aural book, a duet or trio book, some improvisation material, some sight-reading or musical games. Pupils often arrive without their instrument or music and, far from being a problem, this usually presents an opportunity for some fun. But don't make it too much fun or they may never bring their own music!

4

Practice

As an instrumental teacher you should expect your pupils to practise in the same way that they are expected to complete homework for their school lessons. Whilst instrumental lessons are not part of the school curriculum, if a pupil wants to make progress, practice is imperative and as a teacher you are well within your right to make it a compulsory part of your teaching.

Keeping records

Keeping a practice record book in which either you or the pupil can write notes each lesson will help the child to remember exactly what they should be practising and why. It also allows you to write any notes to the parents and gives them a simple way of responding or asking you questions.

For younger pupils a practice chart with boxes, which they should tick when they have practised, is generally very successful. Invest in some star stickers and add them to the chart when work has been achieved.

Don't be afraid to share your own notes with your pupils. Whilst you don't need to show them every comment, the odd relevant fact should alert them to the fact that you will undoubtedly remember what they should have been doing and that they know they can't get away with not doing it! Also by letting them know that you are keeping constant records you may find that they want to do well so that you write positive comments about them.

Managing practice time

The amount of time which pupils should be practising needs to be made clear. I would ask that pupils all schedule five practice sessions a week, for a set amount of time depending on their level of ability. An indication of minimum practice times may be as follows:

Beginner to Grade 2	fifteen minutes
Grade 3	twenty minutes
Grade 4	twenty-five minutes
Grade 5	thirty minutes
Grade 6	forty minutes
Grade 7	forty-five – fifty minutes
Grade 8	an hour

It is important to stress that little and often is far more effective than one big Sunday bash for an hour or more as things often get forgotten by the next session. Try to help them find ways of managing these times, such as putting them in their school homework diary, or speaking to parents to help them organise their time.

Of course every child is different and sometimes they will be able to do more or less than your required amount. In such a case try to find an acceptable middle ground such as swapping five twenty-minutes sessions for three twenty-minutes and one thirty-minutes session.

Remember that your pupil must want to practice to do so. Make sure they have manageable tasks, which can be achieved in the time-scale. Perhaps the pupil could suggest one piece, which they enjoy practising, whilst you suggest another. Any way you can get them to work whilst still achieving their goals is good.

Practice skills

Make sure that your pupils have the skills to do positive and successful practice. Learning how to practice is not easy as once they are alone they will always be tempted to just 'play through'.

Show them how to break down difficult passages, playing slowly and using different rhythms. Encourage them to memorise difficult passages to enable them to get past the difficulty of reading the notes as well coping with the instrument.

Some pupils may need to practice pieces that you have worked on in very small chunks and may struggle with anything too challenging, however others may relish the chance at working something out for themselves and showing off what they can achieve within a week. Find whatever style of practice you think makes that particular pupil motivated to get their instrument out and play it.

Make sure that your pupil knows why they are practising – if they don't understand the aim of what they are doing they are unlikely to be able to focus on it successfully.

Practice structure

Encourage your pupils to start with a warm-up work on a body of pieces then finish with something fun, in the same way that the lesson should have a start, a middle and an end. (see chapter 3.)

School rewards

Find out what reward system the school uses (for example, merit marks), and see if you can tap into it. School reward systems can be extremely useful, and the possibility of earning a merit for learning a set of scales can be a powerful tool!

Lack of practice

Don't be afraid to get a little cross if a pupil has not practised. Whilst it is great to have a fun rapport with your pupil, the most successful teachers are always those who command respect. You will not get this if you do not stand by your word. A request for practice means that you want your pupil to improve and make progress. If they have not done so then you should make it clear that you are disappointed. Rework the practice schedule with them. Work out why they have not completed the work set and find a way of making the next target achievable. Most of all show them that you are serious about wanting them to improve.

In the case of persistent lack of practice it is advisable to discuss their progress with their parents. Make it clear that you have their best interests at heart and you should find that with the help and support of the parents you will get to the root of the problem.

5

Group Lessons

The majority of instrumental teaching in schools is now in the form of the group lesson. This is sadly still viewed as the poor relation to the individual lesson. The almost universally accepted form of instrumental teaching is that of student and master. In this situation the student studies works and performances set by his or her teacher as well as scales and studies, which all work to push him towards a single goal of musical greatness.

A government promise of musical inclusion for all school children led to many pupils being offered the chance to play a musical instrument. However, small budgets and a lack of teachers have meant that the group lesson now has precedence in many county schools. Small bundles of children are ushered into an often tiny teaching room and attempt to learn to blow or scrape a musical instrument for twenty minutes or half an hour. Only those who can afford to pay a little extra may have an individual lesson, either in or outside of school.

Despite prejudices it is often the case that pupils in groups learn faster than those in individual lessons. Many of us teachers will have had the benefit of individual lessons and indeed I can remember having both. I can also remember how lonely it felt when I lost my buddies in my group lesson to go it alone as I had reached the grand old stage of Grade 5. Suddenly I had no one to compare notes with and the only person with the patience to listen to my squeaking, other than my teacher, was my mum. It was about this time that I wanted to give up the clarinet and indeed many pupils do as the pressure of higher grades looms and the work becomes more difficult[2]. Perhaps even at the higher grades there is an argument for keeping a group lesson to share difficulties and provide the pupil with motivation.[3]

The group dynamic

Group teaching, especially in the earlier years, can be great fun and a satisfying challenge for both teacher and pupil. The opportunities for playing together are endless and if the lesson is structured to allow time for fun, as well as time for technique, then the pupils will soon be making quick progress.

Try to make sure that all pupils in a group feel equally valued. Don't let one pupil feel that they are being overlooked or that they are not doing as well as the others. Constantly use positive language equally on all members, highlighting their strengths whilst suggesting ways of improving on their weaknesses.

Ask pupils to teach each other – this will help to reinforce their understanding of topics, as well as help to build a trusting relationship between the pupils and establish a healthy learning environment.

[2] *Thank god for my mum who refused to let me give up until I did my Grade 5 exam which I passed with honours and inspired me to go on and make teaching and playing my career!*

[3] *This should depend on the pupils involved, and the teachers' judgement as to how they will work best.*

As a general rule, most teachers seem to agree that the minimum effective teaching time for a group lesson is thirty minutes. It may be that a slightly larger group in a thirty-minute lesson is better than two smaller ones (although five paying children is the limit in any group lesson).

Don't be afraid to juggle the groups around. The dynamics will change constantly as the pupils get older and develop at different rates. Plus changing groups allows for further development of social skills.

Children of differing abilities

One of the biggest difficulties that music teachers face is that they are forced to teach groups of quite different abilities. In music this is not as big a problem as it might sound but it takes some careful planning by the teacher. Take, for example, three pupils in a small county primary who all want lessons in flute. Their lesson time is twenty minutes, all children started learning together, but each child has progressed differently. There are no other children learning at the same level so it is not possible to switch the groups around. To make it worse, by the time the children arrive for their lesson and set up instruments five minutes of the lesson have gone by. To ensure that they are packed away in time to let the following lesson start on time you need to wrap up the lesson five minutes early. This only leaves ten minutes' quality teaching time. This sounds like an impossible situation, but there are ways of coping.

1 The time issue could be addressed with the class teacher. Many are happy to help if they realise that there is a difficulty and their help may mean your pupils are set up and ready to go while you finish the previous lesson. If cases are left in the classroom the class teacher can make sure instruments are cleaned and packed away. You then regain all of your teaching time.

2 When pupils do arrive they should get themselves organised silently to allow the previous group to finish without distraction.

3 Once you are in the lesson you need to maximise your time. You could ask the more able pupil to watch and help the weaker member of the group, giving them a sense of importance and confidence in their own playing. Weaker pupils often respond well to this kind of help. However, you need to make sure that you don't encourage any attempt at superiority of attitude. If your more able pupil has this tendency then this point will not work!

4 Scales offer an excellent way to involve each child at their own level. Ask the most able to play their scale; perhaps with the next child playing along whilst they watch each other's fingers. They should progress to playing in thirds as above. The child who struggles can play mimins, set against the crotchets or quavers of the other

Further Information

Marks, A ed. (2004), **All Together! Teaching Music in Groups**, London: ABRSM Publishing.

Harris, P and Crozier, R (2000), **The Music Teacher's Companion: A Practical Guide**, London: ABRSM Publishing.

two, creating harmonies, improving tone, intonation and making the scale secure. Many pupils love to hear the harmonies and may start to enjoy their scale practice!

5 Instead of trying to get three pupils to play in tune – why not spend the time trying to get them to play out of tune? They will have great fun with the strange noises that they will make and will strengthen their control of sound in the process.

6 Get pupils to play to each other as if they are looking in a mirror. They should encourage each other to improve posture.

7 Encourage mini concert performances where your pupils suggest ways that they can all improve. The result should be that they are more able to criticise their own practice time.

Mixing groups

Mixing groups can allow a wealth of creative teaching ideas, which are fun and motivating. Try swapping a more able clarinettist with one of a lower ability, or mixing violins and cellos in order to do some ensemble teaching. There are many duet and trio books with exceptionally easy parts set against a more complex melody, which allow for this kind of differentiation. However, this should be a one-off lesson and is not acceptable for any length of time.

Exams

The question of exams can be a difficult issue, when group members are ready at different times and teachers must take a strong line. If a pupil is not ready for an exam – even if another member of a group is entering – the pupil should not enter. If they fail then they will struggle to regain their confidence, especially if they see the other pupil doing well and feel that they can't keep up. Parents can be awkward as they are often an insistent breed – especially if they don't understand musical development. Explain that pupils progress at different rates and that a pupil who may have struggled in an earlier grade often finds that they catch up later. Parents and pupils alike must respect your professional judgement. I have in one case lost a pupil whose parents wanted her to do an exam because her friend was doing one. I refused to enter her, based on the simple fact that she would not pass. The parents found another teacher who did enter her. Sadly the girl failed and soon after gave up playing all together. Had she continued with me, she would have taken the exam at a later date, and whilst she may have still given up, she would hopefully at least have had a better result and would not have had to deal with the negative emotions that come with lack of success.

6

The Right Instrument

Due to limited budgets or availability of teaching staff pupils in primary schools are often only given one or two options of something like flute, clarinet or violin. In secondary schools there is usually more choice but there may still be limitations. The result is that children pick up an instrument according to what is available. If their physiology or temperament is not suited to that instrument they may struggle, eventually become disheartened and give up.

However, it can be much easier than you might think to ensure that pupils start on the right instrument. As a woodwind teacher I have in several cases found myself hauling a bundle of different instruments around to schools to let pupils try to find the one that suits them most. This is of course easier if you are employed by a county music service and have a number of spare instruments available for children to try. I cannot offer every woodwind instrument but I can make a considered guess (NB see chapter 2 for advice on teaching instruments other than your own). A nice, strong, even tone at first blow usually indicates that the child may do well.

If an appropriate instrument is not found then a visit by a teacher of a different instrumental group should come next. Suggest, as a bargaining tool, the fact that at any such visit there are usually a number of young musicians who want to start learning. That could be the start of a whole new musical area for your county or school. Perhaps one-off workshops could be arranged with a view to encouraging pupils to start when they reach the senior school or else encouraging the parents to find a private teacher.

Whilst you should look at physical features, such as the development of adult teeth and size of hands, I would not suggest making judgments about appropriate instruments based solely on physical shape. There are many successful musicians who have the supposed wrong 'shape' for their instrument. In fact, despite physiology still being a popular measure when choosing an instrument, research suggests it is irrelevant. Janet Mills (2005) proved that children with any kind of physical characteristics can do well if they are motivated and well taught. Therefore if a child with fat lips has a strong desire to play the flute then they should be allowed to do so.

If a pupil has already got his or her own instrument but you feel that they would do better on a different one, then you have a bigger but not insurmountable problem. The likelihood is that they will probably have been playing for a while but perhaps they have not made much progress. Firstly, you need to get parents on your side. Get permission to allow their child to try other instruments, explaining why you think it is necessary. Reassure them that if you find that they are more suited to another instrument there are ways of changing it without forking out lots more money, such as part-exchanging it, selling it privately or perhaps even swapping an instrument with another pupil.

If there is no other way than to continue with the instrument which they already have, then try to give them as much encouragement as possible. Progress can always be made, however small, and sometimes a pupil who seems to be learning the totally wrong instrument can suddenly make good progress and turn into a fine musician. Stay positive, creative, and find as many ways as possible of ensuring that they continue to enjoy their musical involvement.

Further Information

Mills, J (2005), **Music in the School**, Oxford: Oxford University Press.

7

Learning Styles

It is generally accepted these days that there is no such thing as a non-musical child. Each child will have their own personal experience of music, which they bring to their lessons. We as teachers should tap into and develop this experience, using it to build and shape their instrumental progress. It is by building on their previous knowledge and understanding that we can find and nurture their confidence and motivation.

How the brain works

Children learn through, not about, music. The physical activity of making and hearing music is how they develop as musicians. During the process of learning we need to access two sides of the brain. Understanding this can be fundamental to the way you teach and your pupils' consequent progression.

The right brain

The right brain is the artistic side. Children who have a dominant right brain tend to make an overall impression of a piece before absorbing any technical details. New music is learnt holistically with a strong aural element. Imagination and expression are first and foremost. Right-sided learners may find analysis difficult. They may well need to hear the piece in its entirety before they can understand it and play it successfully.

The left brain

The left brain is the analytical side. People who have a dominant left brain have a much more methodical way of exploring the world. New music will be learnt piecemeal, starting with technical details and providing an overall impression later. It is a visual learning style rather than an aural. Pupils who have a dominant left brain will first want to know exactly how to play the notes before they consider how to express them. They will find analytical methods of learning easy. They need to get involved with the detailed analysis of the work. These learners are often visual learners and are best at sight-reading.

It is only after the initial learning process has started that the two sides start to work together.

Kinesthetic learning

Some pupils learn kinesthetically which means they learn through the physical action of playing the notes. For example, they learn to play scales through the fingering patterns rather than learning the notes. They will probably need lots of slow repetition to learn a piece successfully but once it is learnt it will not be easily forgotten.

How to bring different learning styles together

If you can identify your pupils learning style, you can adapt your teaching style accordingly. However, all pupils' need to develop ways of improving their weaker sides to be a fully successful musician. Right-brained learners need to improve their analytical side to be able to sight-read, whilst left-brained learners need to develop their creative side to be able to improvise successfully. Try some of the following to bring the two together:

• Slow a piece down to allow your pupil to play with no mistakes. This will allow them to gain complete control. This should eliminate the wild fluctuations in tempo which pupils get by trying to move quicker than they are able.

• Try separating elements such as playing hands apart, learning a phrase at a time or moving fingers without an instrument in hand. This can help a right-brained pupil to think about detailed technique and can help a kinesthetic learner to gain control of the piece.

• Make a separate score of dynamics to help to encourage a left-brained pupil to think expressively.

8

Learning Difficulties

Music is an important subject for any child with learning disabilities as it is a subject which offers inclusion to a huge degree. The joy of learning a musical instrument has many benefits, from improving co-ordination and cognitive skills to the social benefits of being part of an ensemble. Even the simple task of playing a steady crotchet beat on a tambourine may give the child who often struggles with school work or social skills the confidence to play in an ensemble.

When you start teaching in a school or have a new pupil you should always ask to have access to the special needs register. Important information should be available to you but it is not always forthcoming unless you ask for it.

However, problems are not always identified early on and often it is an instrumental music teacher in a short but intensive music lesson who spots problems that a classroom teacher may take longer to notice. You should always look for signs such as constant questioning, a lack of understanding, confused fingerings, showing indifference or aggression: these can all point to learning difficulties of some kind.

If you suspect a learning difficulty you should speak to the school music teacher, who will involve the SENCO (Special Education Needs Co-ordinator). They will observe the pupil in other lessons, assess the requirements of the pupil and establish the level of any special educational needs. If possible you should try to remain in contact with the SENCO and ensure that you have a chance to speak to them directly at regular intervals. They are a good source of information regarding all manner of learning difficulties and usually have plenty of literature, which may help you to understand the pupil further. There are many different ways of coping with such conditions and often these children are inherently musical, simply needing understanding and patience. Where to find information and how to access it both in and out of school is vital.

The person who knows the child best is the parent. It may help to speak to them and agree on what is expected of the lessons. Don't be afraid to ask questions regarding the child's condition – remember that they are the experts on their child; you are the expert on your instrument. If a certain method of learning or activity is inappropriate for the child it must be broached, either by the teacher or parent because the child may not always find it easy to be honest about their condition.

Down Syndrome

Down Syndrome is a learning difficulty that can in some ways be dealt with more easily than others, as there can be no hiding from it. Those affected are generally extremely caring and happy in what they do and will aim to please both you and themselves. A frank discussion needs to be had with the parent or carer and all communication should be with them and not with the pupil.

In general some symptoms include poor muscle tone and co-ordination, health problems and a lower IQ than those children of a similar age. Don't underestimate the creative learning ability of Down Syndrome children or the joy they will gain from learning a new skill, however basic it may seem to you. Just playing a few simple tunes from memory will give them great joy, although they may progress far further than this. There should be an improvement in their general motor skills as a result of practicing the co-ordination needed to play an instrument.

Autism

Autism is an interesting area for music teachers, as children who have some form of autism are often extremely creative. Their difficulty is reacting to and understanding other people. They take comments literally and your main concern as a teacher is watching what you say and how you say it. Be clear about what you want them to do but remember to use encouraging language. Don't use language that belittles their skills in anyway, even if you mean the opposite, as words can be taken extremely literally. Also do not get fazed by unusual comments, autistic people speak as they find, and this can be disconcerting.

Dyslexia

Instrumental teachers often encounter dyslexia, sometimes known as 'word blindness', not least because, as with other learning difficulties, those who have the condition often have a strong artistic side. At first they may appear dozy, lazy or show a lack of concentration. This is not generally the case and if you are aware of their condition then you need to change tack quite dramatically. If you are not aware that they have any form of dyslexia then perhaps you may be able to help identify it.

Understanding the difficulties which may be encountered are key. They are usually specific to what is seen on the page, including:

- Notes appearing to jump between spaces and lines on the page, with particular difficulty when notes are close together e.g. b and c.

- Notes may disappear or new notes may be seen which aren't on the page.

- There will be a great deal of difficulty in understanding the difference between treble and bass clef.

- Following movement along a page is difficult.

- Assimilation of key, together with rhythm and note reading, may be almost impossible at first attempt, therefore sight-reading will be a particular problem. Don't be surprised if they make it up and make a good job of it! These children are often very creative and may well have a good ear!

Some ways of dealing with the problems include:

- One of the best ways to rectify this is the use of a coloured film over the music – these are available in most good stationers. The choice of colour can be vital and it is not a bad idea to carry a pack of several colours to experiment with.

- Photocopy the music onto coloured paper (although yellow seems to be unpopular).

- Enlarge the score as this allows the notes to settle on the page.

- Your pupil may well have an exceptionally good long-term memory and they will commit things to memory to save having to read them. Use this to advantage!

- Be ready with spare copies of their music, or alter native lesson ideas, as dyslexic pupils can be very disorganized. Firmly remind them to bring forgotten music next lesson but in the meantime ensure that you have other activities planned.

- Use mnemonics as you would with beginners – be prepared to work them out with the pupil to find words which they will best remember. Have a different system for treble and bass clefs e.g. food in the bass (Great Buns do Fatten All and All Chips End Greasy) and sport in the treble (Every Good Boy Deserves Football and Footballers Are Careful Eaters) as these can be easily confused.

- Break down pieces into small sections and memorise short passages, (but be aware that starting in the middle of a piece, which has been learnt from memory, may cause additional problems).

- Experiment using letters instead of notation. This will help to reinforce note learning, and although time-consuming, if you can write music out using letters on the stave with note tails, then this will help them to understand notation more easily.

It is vital to pick up on these cases as the danger is that the pupil may continue through their school life always 'getting by' and often hiding their difficulty. Help is usually readily available and schools are becoming more and more aware of exactly what methods are most appropriate. Incredibly, around 10% of children may suffer from some form of dyslexia.

Dyspraxia

This is often linked to dyslexia but the difficulty is hand and eye co-ordination and spatial awareness. Recognising a dyspraxic child is similar to identifying a dyslexic, however, they may well also have a messy physical appearance as tasks such as putting on a tie will be difficult. They may get left and right or horizontal and vertical muddled up and the spatial complications involved in looking at a vertical plane but playing a horizontal instrument will be difficult.

There are other conditions such as ADHD, Aspergers Syndrome and BED which have not been mentioned here. Always speak to the SENCO for advice. The following are some general rules which apply to all children with learning difficulties.

General rules for teaching children with special needs

- Always remain calm – this seems obvious but it can be frustrating when a pupil does not seem to understand something that you think you have explained quite clearly. Remember that the brain may process things more slowly and in a different way to other children and lots of repetition will be necessary.

- Building confidence is key and you need to have total belief in your pupils' ability – even when you feel annoyed or frustrated. Feelings are infectious and any loss of patience on your part will be communicated to the pupil.

- Never rush – even when you can feel the time restraint of the lesson.

- Use language carefully – 'take your time', 'you can do it!', 'don't worry about that mistake – you fixed this one and you will get both bits right after a bit more practice!'.

- Try to always speak to someone who has a close knowledge of the child and who knows what tactics do and don't work. Use their information as a general guide but also find your own ways of getting your point across in the lessons.

- If a pupil is making slow progress don't worry. They will be gaining huge enjoyment out of simply coming to a lesson with a teacher who gives them their total concentration for half an hour. If this is all that is achieved during the lesson, then rest assured that you have helped that pupil build confidence and self-esteem. Whilst this may not always equate musical progress, it may well equate huge progress of another kind.

- If a tactic is not working then feel free to try some thing else. This is a chance for some creative teaching and by trying new ideas, not only will your pupil find your lessons refreshing and fun but you may well find the key to unlocking their musical ability which traditional methods may not.

Further Information

Melody provides help, support and ideas for teachers, parents and carers, **www.melody.me.uk**

The British Dyslexia Association 98 London Road, Reading, RG1 5AU, 0118 966 8271, **www.bda-dyslexia.org.uk** or email: **info@dyslexiahelp-bda.demon.uk**

National Music and Disability Information, **info@soundsense.org**

National Down Syndrome Society, www.ndss.org or Down Syndrome Educational Trust, **www.downsed.org**

National Autistic Society, **www.nas.org**

British Institute of Learning Disabilities, **www.bild.org.uk**

• Don't promise things that you cannot fulfil. As with very young children a promise is made to keep and you will lose the trust that your pupil has in you if you can not fulfil your promises. You are in a very privileged and trusted position, and you may find yourself a confidant for your pupil.[4]

• Don't change your routine if you can help it. Even something like a change of room can have a damaging effect on a pupil with learning difficulties. Although things like this are often out of our control, try to maintain as much routine as you can throughout each lesson.

• Don't ask a pupil to do things that are beyond his or her capability or overload them with new information. Confidence will need to be encouraged through very small and manageable chunks. This may seem slow to you but rest assured that it can seem speedy to your pupil.

• If a child has difficulty with reading and writing they will probably find it difficult to learn to read music. Use your judgment and experimentation to get the level of learning right, starting with the most basic and working upwards. But make sure you don't rely on written music, encourage learning by ear and improvisation.

• For all children with co-ordination difficulties a large instrument with lots of finger space, limited strings or valves may help.

• Capitalise on what the pupil can do well to ensure a feeling of success, whilst broadening their knowledge of areas that they can do less well.

• It can help if a parent or carer can attend the lesson and help with practice during the week. Perhaps an after-school lesson may facilitate this. Even if this can't happen on a regular basis, a few lessons in this way may provide a boost for the pupil and will help you and the parent / carer gain a fuller understanding of both their own role and the pupil's learning ability.

The positive effects of music can be profound. Several years ago I had a pupil with ADHD. Most teachers at her school found that she was rude, disruptive and would not engage in any activity. She had very few friends. By experimenting with 'making up tunes' she was soon improvising through some simple but effective chord structures. Bumping into her four years after she left school all she could talk about was how much fun she had in her saxophone lessons and how she was enjoying playing with a local jazz band who let her just join in and play by ear, and with who she also met socially once or twice a week. Her lessons at school allowed her not only to develop as a musician but gave her a focus when she left school and enabled her to develop social skills that she may have otherwise struggled to attain.

[4] *NB. If you do find that your pupil confides in you something of a personal nature you are required to let someone in school know. Therefore if you are in this position you must be honest with the child, but reassure them that it will be dealt with as sensitively as possible.*

9

Gifted and Talented

Sometimes in our careers we are lucky enough to come across those pupils who shine in a very special and talented way. Often this talent emerges in the very young – up to about age five; but it can also appear at any time, especially with wind players who do not generally start playing until they are a few years older.

Spotting a gifted child is often left to the teacher who sees them in a specifically musical environment. The child may have certain characteristics such as a highly active imagination, a high level of intelligence and an ability to focus on tasks with motivation and application unusual in a child of their age.

Their sense of musicianship will be keen – aural awareness such as knowledge of pitch will usually be quite advanced and they will have a steady and secure sense of rhythm. They will probably also be quite expressive and be able to shape phrases musically, even in the early stages.

If you find yourself teaching a gifted child it is important to consider whether you are the right teacher – for example, if bassoon is your second instrument are you really a strong enough practitioner of that instrument to teach the child to the highest level. If the answer is no then you must not be afraid to admit it and to help the parents or school to find a more appropriate teacher or even a specialist school.

You may find that if you do continue with the child, there may come a point where their technique or level of expression is beyond your own. Don't feel intimidated but be proud that you were part of their musical education and help them on to the next level, whether that is finding a new teacher or even just organising a few lessons with another teacher.

I often send my Grade 8 and diploma pupils to another teacher, as a matter of course, as it gives them a different perspective. When they return with fresh ideas it also tends to enhance my own teaching and we can continue together with renewed vigour, enthusiasm and confidence.

From a practical point of view, parents need to be aware of the potential of the child, as well as the potential costs. Lessons, an appropriate instrument, music courses etc. can all have a crippling financial effect and may require some considerable financial planning.

When teaching gifted and talented pupils you may find that they pick up technical points quickly and accurately and you can put more emphasis on expression and communication. Try encouraging them to play their pieces in different keys, developing their inner ear as far as possible.

Musical memory is important, as this is imperative in encouraging creative performance. Memorising passages of music takes away reliance on the notated score and allows free creative expression.

In-depth work on interpretation will be possible, even in the early grades. Encourage pupils to experiment with the effect of changing dynamics and articulation and justify their choices. Creating a dynamics only score will enhance their awareness of how to use dynamics expressively. If they make their own decisions about stylistic elements, not only are they increasing their stylistic awareness, but they are much more likely to remember and include them in any performance.

Encourage your pupil to sing their pieces. The voice is the most natural of instruments and moving away from the restraints of keys or strings can open up a wealth of free expression. For those who are unsure of themselves vocally, suggest they sing in the shower – the acoustics are great!

Don't be tempted to push them forward with pages of studies. Some of the best technical exercises look like wallpaper and whilst their benefits cannot be denied they can demoralise and flatten a pupil's enthusiasm dead. Choose studies which aid the development of a piece – for example use a staccato study when faced with some tough tonguing passages in an orchestral extract.

Don't feel like you need to do every exam with them; gifted pupils will fly through grades more quickly than others and you don't want to hamper their progress or stem their enthusiasm by working through list after list of exam repertoire. Use festivals and competitions as benchmarks and the exams which are relevant and which the pupil really wants to do.

Encourage them to research the piece or composer. Knowing details of the composer's state of mind as he was writing can greatly change how a piece is perceived. The internet provides an easy way of obtaining information and recordings and can greatly enhance a performance. It is also excellent preparation for diploma examinations or recitals where programme notes will be required.

Most of all encourage their confidence and creativity. They need your support more strongly than most and you may find yourself in close and constant contact with the family. Ensure that you are always challenging and stimulating your pupil in new and inspiring ways and look out for any signs of boredom. Enjoy your time with them and they will certainly enjoy having lessons with you.

Further Reading

Ed. Harris P and Crozier R (2000), **The Music Teacher's Companion**, London: ABRSM Publishing.

10

Exams - or not?

Graded music exams, for teachers, parents and pupils alike, often become the be all and end all of learning a musical instrument. But are they even necessary?

In some countries exams are even frowned upon, the belief being that they slow a child's progression rather than enhance it, hindering natural creativity by tying the child to a diet of prescribed pieces, instead of letting them explore new styles and genres.

When children reach high grades at an early age, it is questionable as to whether students have the musical maturity required for Grade 8. At this level a high degree of musicianship, understanding and all round performance is required which a younger child is unlikely to possess – no matter how fantastic their technical ability is.

Some kind of compromise is required. Exams can give students a benchmark, which allows them to see how they are developing. It provides an aim, encouragement and rewarding success, which in turn drives the student on. It should never be a long slog of uninspired list pieces.

Parental pressure

One problem often encountered by teachers is the parental desire for their offspring to complete a grade a year. This attitude is particularly prevalent in private schools where the pressure to achieve can be extremely high. Explaining that students achieve at different rates is not always easily understood. Take little Amelia who has been playing for four years but is only just taking her Grade 2. Best friend Eleanor has been playing for only two years, is the same age, but has taken her Grade 3 and was awarded a distinction. Amelia's parents don't understand why she appears to be behind her friend and the teacher is put under pressure to push progress on beyond its natural state. The reality may be that Eleanor was able to pick up her instrument and learn quickly but Amelia's fingers were not quite big enough to allow her to play confidently. However, this should not reduce the value of those two extra years in which Amelia was learning. She will have gained a sound musical knowledge as well as enjoyment and the confidence of playing in school concerts or other events.

The music

The need to do each and every grade is unnecessary. The three times a year exam dates do not always tie in with a students readiness to enter an exam and in such a case it may be more beneficial to simply continue on to the next grade without pause, allowing time to explore new and exciting repertoire along the way.

The use of 'unprescribed' works is important. Students may get tired of exams and exam pieces. Chamber music, or music in different styles, may improve a pupil's technique far more quickly than hanging around on the same pieces for several terms, as they will provide something new and inspiring. If you are working for exams, trying out lots of pieces on the list is highly advisable. What suits one child may not suit another and even in the early grades it is important that the right pieces are found for each individual. The aspect of choice is also very important for children as it allows them to take more responsibility for their own progress, which in turn will encourage them to practice and improve. A word about the job of the examiner is also relevant here; listening to an afternoon of Grade 1 clarinettists all playing the same pieces can be tedious to say the least. Finding pieces that suit the pupil will make each performance individual and interesting and make for a much nicer day for all involved!

Keep your teaching fresh

Returning to the music itself, it is important for teachers themselves to use music that varies from the exam norm. For a teacher to remain fresh with an aware and interesting teaching style, they must themselves remain inspired. A life-time of studies and prescribed pieces will not do this.

One way of getting around this is by trying something new like the jazz syllabi. This does not cover all instruments but Trinity-Guildhall, London College and the ABRSM all offer a comprehensive jazz syllabus for woodwind and piano.

I first tried a jazz syllabus with a pupil who wanted to try something a little different and who was willing to be a guinea pig! A little honesty with parents goes a long way; don't pretend to be something you are not. If parents and pupils have trust in your ability as a teacher they will know that you will do whatever is required to become familiar enough with the syllabus to make it successful. There must always be a first time! In fact my pupil was quite honoured that I trusted her abilities enough to try this new musical adventure.

Scales and aural

Whether you are working from a syllabus or not the need to continue scales and aural work is vital. Pupils often ask – 'Why do we need to play scales? They're so boring!'. They need to understand the role in improving tone and control of the instrument, as well as the fact that they are learning the basis of all the music that they will ever play. Try different ways of learning scales. Improvisation can be a fun way of exploring a scale or playing in thirds with the teacher or another pupil. There are lots of fun books around which encourage interesting use of scales – suggest the pupil go and choose their own. Again the ownership issue of choosing something, which is going to improve their playing, may help. And anything that puts an end to last minute panic practice over scales has to be a good thing!

The same goes for aural work. The more a pupil is encouraged to sing and listen, the less they will feel intimidated by it when it comes around to exam time. It should be a normal part of the lesson. Use the opening or ending of a lesson to work on the exam tests and make sure that they are familiar with the terminology and phrasing that the examiner will use.

Performing issues such as intonation should be improved with aural work, through listening to and singing intervals, and short passages. This will help to gain a deeper overall awareness of the pieces they are playing and music in general. See Chapter 12 on supporting skills.

Exam management

The student needs to be well prepared for how the exam is actually managed by the examiner. Examiners work within a limited timescale and whilst they generally ensure that the candidate is comfortable and at ease, this can be difficult when pupils are unprepared, bundling their way through tuning difficulties which could have been fixed outside the room or being unaware of what they will be asked to do.

The best way of approaching this is to do a mock exam, using appropriate language and correct time-scales.

Accompanying exams

The best advice I can give about accompanying exams – and this is aimed at teachers who worry about their piano playing not being up to scratch – is to start with early grades and give it a go! You need to make sure you have practiced like mad because it can be easy to make a simple mistake, which can in turn have a terrible effect on the candidate. But at the end of the day, a pupil would always rather have their own teacher with them, who they have rehearsed with and who they feel 'safe' with, rather than an unknown pianist, no matter how good they may be.

This is of course truer of the early grades and by Grade 7 and 8 it is entirely acceptable to use an accompanist (some of these pieces challenge even the most accomplished pianist!). However, if you can learn a few of the early grade pieces, you could accompany your most confident pupils which will in turn give you the confidence to do more.

Be honest with the parents. They will appreciate your honesty and will know their child well enough to realise that they would probably rather 'risk' using you than use someone unknown. If you have been honest and you have practiced enough you will feel relaxed enough to do a good job.

At the end of the day you are not the one being examined and your only role is to support your pupil. If you can't reach that octave and a half stretch then don't try. It's far more important that you are able to follow the candidate securely, jumping bars with them if necessary, and holding a steady and safe accompaniment to their performance. Just remember that whatever you have practiced with them in their lessons you must play in the exam, so if you have played a simplified version to 'get by', then don't try and change it for the exam! That said you must be as true to the music as you can, so if the music really is beyond you then perhaps you are not ready for this exam. Try and be ready for the next one.

This chapter formed the basis of an article in 'Music Teacher', September 2005.

11

Report Writing

Around once a year a dreaded task is required from instrumental music teachers. It puts fear into our hearts and turns our hand to a jellied blob. This is the time for writing reports!

Even if all your pupils are delightful and practice regularly, writing reports can be difficult. Trying to say relevant and informative things about each individual can be tough, especially if you have many pupils working in group lessons or of similar standards.

Try to use varied language and be creative with the phrases you choose. Making a note of useful phrases can be helpful so that when you get stuck (usually by around the twentieth report!) you have some inspiration.

However, if you do have a supply of stock words and phrases, use them wisely. For example, 'works well in his lessons' could be true of both the child who does no practice outside of this time and is making slow progress, and the child who also works well at home and is rapidly becoming an exceptional musician. What is important is how you qualify your statement. A balance of positive comments and constructive criticism should be used to do this in each report. Not easy when you often have only a tiny box to write in!

Use positive language. 'Steve is making no progress because he doesn't practice' may be a true statement but to gain the support and understanding of the parents it needs some positive reinforcement or clarification such as 'but he does work well in the lessons.' You could then suggest a realistic practice schedule, thus making the parents aware of what their child needs to do to improve (something which parents are often unaware of).

Occasionally it can be difficult to find suitable positive comments but encouraging language is vital. If your pupil thinks you have nothing good to say they will be unlikely to do any more work for your lessons. Even a short comment on good punctuality may do the trick!

Be wary of including too much technical language, which a non-musical parent won't be familiar with. Parents get suspicious if they are bombarded with unknown words and phrases such as 'embouchure'. They want to know how their child is progressing in layman's terms. However, don't insult their intelligence either, even the most non-musical parent can work out the meaning of 'poor tone' or 'good rhythmic skills'.

When you have pupils who are musically gifted and who work well, you need to reflect this but also remember that they also need some constructive criticism. No one is perfect and you don't want them to think that they don't need to practice. Always comment on areas that need improvement as well as areas of success.

Depending on the school or music service, sometimes you find you have a set style of report form. As a general rule those produced for music services allow more space whilst school forms can be restrictive. You must, in both cases, try to include as much information as possible to provide a balanced account of progress. Most of all it is important to be honest. This is often the only contact that parents get from you and they need a clear picture of their child's progress. Parents are often present when their child practices and getting parents on side, with a clear understanding of what is needed for musical improvement, is invaluable.

Keeping clear notes throughout the year is invaluable to enable you to write a true and reflective report. It helps to organise your notes into pupil files rather than teaching days. This requires a bit more thought than simply keeping a weekly notebook but is well worth it for lots of reasons. If you can afford it, invest in an iPAQ or pocketword notebook which you can use to keep notes and separate files on. It has the added benefit of allowing you to copy notes directly into the report (unless they are handwritten), and minimises the paperwork that you need to carry between schools – especially valuable in our profession where carrying heavy instruments and music is normal. For this reason a laptop is not generally as practical although it can also be incredibly useful if you are based in just one place.

In this day and age more and more record keeping is necessary. With new shifts of money away from Instrumental Music Services direct to schools, our jobs are being taken more seriously and teachers are finding that they are subject to ever-increasing checks. In one music school in the Midlands, reports are required once a term in addition to a separate report held by the school. Heads of Music are observing their instrumental staff to a much higher degree. Parents are far more pro-active in trying to understand their children's education and what exactly they are getting for their money.

In this climate it is vital that we stay ahead of the game. We need to have up to date records and justify our teaching practice constantly. Different schools and music services require different levels of this kind of administration and it can often seem bureaucratic and unnecessary. However, administration has massive benefits; by completing these tasks, report writing becomes one small part for which we are fully prepared, and which will reflect a positive and successful teaching basis.

12

Supporting Skills

Supporting skills such as aural, sight-reading, scales and improvisation are often left to the last minute. The productive part of the lesson is spent focussing on pieces, with supporting skills tagged on the end. These skills are then not so much learned as the pupil is simply made aware of their existence. The result is often a fear and lack of understanding, and poor results in exams. The following is a few suggestions for redressing this balance.

Sight-reading

To be a strong sight-reader is to ensure lifelong enjoyment as a successful musician. It aids a free sense of musical awareness as it releases the shackles of struggling with 'reading the dots'.

Although there is always a debate as to whether you can actually teach sight-reading, my feeling is that you can teach the skills required – the rest is then down to encouragement and building confidence in the pupil.

The most important thing is to make sure that they have a thorough understanding of pulse and rhythm. It is this more than note-reading, which brings down exam results. Pupils should work out a pulse and demonstrate it to ensure that they are feeling it physically and correctly. Ask them to count a few bars aloud to allow you to check they have a steady pulse at an appropriate speed. Tapping the rhythm with one hand whilst tapping the pulse with their foot can be effective, although difficult at first. Practice reading rhythmic patterns, perhaps using flash cards or sight-reading books, all of which are available from most music shops. Clap the rhythm first as this will help them to feel the pulse more clearly and to play more fluently when they try to combine the rhythm with notes.

As for the notes, a strongly developed sense of key is vital. Generally speaking, it seems that the sight-reading keys are close to those studied in the exam lists, therefore if you cover a reasonable amount of repertoire, and your pupil has learnt their scales, they should be able to remember a key signature easily and should be able to cope with any relevant fingering difficulties.

Once you have dealt with the basic rhythm and note combination, then they must cope with thinking about the time signature, dynamics, and any fingering difficulties. Make sure that they are used to reading ahead and take notice of the dynamics. Try to encourage them to hear the sounds in their head. Some exam boards insist on silent preparation for the sight-reading test and this can often produce much more successful results. By having to look at the pieces silently they have no choice but to imagine what it will sound like. Also, trying to work something out away from the instrument allows the brain to focus on one thing at a time, therefore when the piece is played it generally has more fluency than when the pupil 'tries it out' beforehand.

Of course the danger is that your pupil will 'hear' it incorrectly and may be thrown off course when they hear it. The trick here is to practice so that even if they hear the notes wrongly they are able to keep to the rhythm. Eventually they will be able to do this with confidence.

When they have played a piece of sight-reading ask them to comment on their performance. If they can pick out mistakes they are much more likely to get them right in the future than if you pick them out. Ask them to play it again and see if they can correct it second time around.

Of course one of the most fun ways to practice sight-reading is by playing duets, trios and other ensembles where the pupil has to keep moving to keep up with the other part or parts.

Scales

Scales are not generally viewed with much enthusiasm! However, giving your pupils a working understanding of why they are important can make all the difference. Get them to list all the reasons why they should practice them. Then compare it with your own reasons. It should include:

- It promotes a sound sense of key.

- It helps hugely with sight-reading and learning new pieces.

- It improves finger dexterity and general control of the instrument.

- It improves tone production throughout the range of the instrument.

- It will allow the pupil to gain good marks in exams.

Note that 'good marks in exams' is presented as the last point – exactly where it should be!

Technique for learning scales

- Practice the scales, which are relevant to the pieces being studied, including major, minor and any other related scale. This will help to shape an understanding of the music.

- Always point out scale or arpeggio passages in pieces of music.

- Improvise on the scale being used in as many different styles as you can!

- Use rhythmic patterns to make them more interesting and gain an even finger control.

- Use scales to work on intonation – try playing them in thirds or fifths with another pupil.

- Try practicing from different points in the scale, such as the top or the fifth to get a feel for the key.

- Vary the articulation.

- Make sure that your pupils actually know which scales they are playing and don't just find them by accident. To be successful they need to understand the scale fully.

- Devise short snippets to make sure that you work on any difficult fingering bits – especially when working on melodic minors.

Aural skills

Aural skills are often the worst prepared for exams. Teachers often prepare only what is necessary to gain a pass in the exam. However, a keen sense of aural awareness leads to improved intonation, communication and reading skills. As a general rule it is important to include aural work throughout each lesson as you work through each piece.

Aural tests

- Try to encourage listening for certain melodies when recognising intervals, e.g. a major third is the opening of the Christmas carol 'While Shepherds Watched Their Flock By Night'.

- Identify cadences in pieces learnt as well as any sight-reading tests to help to practice recognition of cadences.

- Use 'happy' and 'sad' to describe major and minor.

- Encourage pupils to use descriptive language so that they have the literary skills to describe changes in descriptive questions and viva voce.

- When singing back melodies or clapping back a rhythm, start with short and easy tests – several grades lower than required if necessary – to establish confidence before working up to harder tests.

- Make obvious mistakes in pieces and encourage your pupils to spot them.

- Discuss difficult rhythms in any of the tests, and compare them to pieces that they already know.

Improvisation

To be able to improvise is to gain a freedom and fluency throughout our whole playing skill. It can aid a sense of musicianship, through developing musical creativity. However, improvisation is often feared by teachers and pupils alike. Some of the following ideas may enable you to explore the possibilities of improvising:

- Use question and answer, starting with simple two bar rhythmic phrases and build up to include cadences and key changes.

- Use simple well-known melodies and try to change the endings e.g. 'Twinkle Twinkle Little Star'.

- Play notes in response to colours e.g. red may encourage angry, fiery sounds.

- Play notes in response to shapes – perhaps drawing a line and following its highs and lows.

- Practice scales in response to mood e.g. develop a tune in E minor to suggest a sad mood.

- Provide a set of notes – as few as three or an entire scale over several octaves depending on ability – and use a simple ostinato accompaniment for them to improvise over.

Singing and vocal skills

Pupils can be very reticent about singing – maybe due to shyness, or changing voices, or a fear of getting it wrong. But there are ways to encourage them.

- Try getting them to sing parts of their pieces – this will have the dual effect of allowing them to increase their vocal confidence and help them express the piece more fully. But make sure that they are singing within their range as struggling for notes will have the opposite effect and can destroy their confidence.

- Encourage open-mouthed sounds such as 'la' or 'ah' or even 'nn' instead of humming, which can be less defined and therefore lead to mistakes more easily.

- When working on pieces, identify intervals and ask them to sing the same interval on different notes. Ask them to sing passages of sight-reading – e.g. a scale or arpeggio passage.

- Use question and answer phrases in the same way you might to encourage improvisation on an instrument.

- Most of all, try to make it fun!

Obviously none of the above are exhaustive and you will doubtless find many more ways to develop all the supporting skills required to be a successful musician.

13

Musical Games

Development as a musician requires many skills. Communication, co-ordination, numeracy and literacy are among just a few. A balanced diet of pieces, scales and performances will give a major push in the right direction. But there are other stimulating ways of furthering development.

Putting the instrument down and trying musical games can be daunting. However, this is an extremely effective way of enhancing musical awareness as well as being great fun! We only need look at the world of sport where it is easy to see how games with a ball as a young child are an excellent preparation for many types of ball sports in later life, developing hand-to-eye co-ordination, balance, strength and teamwork. In the same way musical games vastly improve general musicianship.

Here is a look at some key areas with appropriate games to try. They work well either as a warm-up to a lesson or as a fun ending. You will find that some will work better than others. The key is trial and error – remember, if you enjoy them, your pupils will find them both fun and progressive.

The following games are designed to improve aural skills.

The Shopping Game
(sometimes known as 'My Grandmother's Chest') – for three plus players. This is the same as the memory game where one person starts a shopping list then each person adds a new item. In the musical version the starting line 'I went to shops today and I bought…' is sung and each new item is given a note. As the list is passed around, the pitch should be remembered as well as the item, developing musical memory and pitch.

Scale games
Give a keynote and chord. Ask each person to sing a degree of the scale. If there is just one person then the aim is to get the note as quickly as possible. If there are more people then the game can be extended to include held chords and dynamics, adding a dimension of breath control to the game.

Another good exercise is to sing scales in thirds. One person should start a scale and the next starts two notes later. This is excellent aural preparation and is especially effective when using minor keys. It can be developed by using a conductor who indicates the direction of the scale.

Singing games
Singing games are especially useful for pupils who are not used to singing. They are generally easier in a group, although can be fun with any number of people.

• Rounds of any kind work well; simple songs such as 'London's Burning' are fine. Next, try using two songs together such as 'It's a Long Way to Tipperary' and 'Pack Up Your Troubles' (my Gran taught me those, and my toddler loves them!).

• Sing or play a melody and improvise an ending over a set number of bars. If the students are of higher grades they can finish with a cadence relevant to the aural tests at that grade.

A sense of rhythm and pulse is the single most important area to develop and can be the most difficult. Rhythmic games allow musical time to become clear without the added difficulty of playing notes and worrying about what fingers / breath / posture etc. are supposed to be doing. They are particularly useful when looking at new concepts – from simple subdivision to complicated time signatures and syncopation. In addition to those listed below, the range of sight-reading books available often includes clapping exercises and these are invaluable.

Echoes
The teacher claps a rhythm and the pupil claps it back. The pupil can then clap a rhythm for the teacher or another pupil.

Clapping rhymes
This is a simple game where the teacher claps the rhythm of a nursery rhyme and the pupil has to guess what it is. It can be made more complicated by clapping only the first line of the rhyme. The answer should be given by way of a clapped or sung ending.

Understanding note values
This is more effective in a group but can be done with just pupil and teacher.

Start by asking everyone to clap crotchets. Change to quavers, then minims etc. When this has been achieved, ask one pupil to clap crotchets whilst another claps quavers. Change the note values of each group on a signal, encouraging them to work as a team. Then try giving each group a pattern to clap, swapping on the teacher's or an appointed director's signal.

Adding game
Write some musical sums on a piece of manuscript or show your pupils how to do this. Then ask them to add them up – e.g. two crotchets = a minim. From here they could do sums for each other. Encourage them to be as creative as possible. This also works as mental arithmetic and is a good warm-up to sight-reading.

Note: recognition is relevant to all instruments as well as general theory. This next game can be used with or without an instrument.

Musical spelling

The teacher 'spells' a word on the stave – e.g. DAD, BAD or DEAD, which the pupil then must recognise by either saying the word or by playing it. Encourage the pupils to spell words for each other, giving points for the most creative.

Spelling as composition

Use spelling notes as a method of composing. Start by asking your pupils to play three random notes, then get them to write them down (on the stave or just letter names is fine). Next see how they can make a word. This can be quite satifying as it is or could be developed even further, using the 'word' as a motif and playing forwards, backwards, high, low, loud, soft etc. Add another 'word' to see if the two can fit together. The possibilities are endless!

Physical development is vital if a pupil is to gain a smooth command of their instrument. In many cases this can involve unnatural postures or positions. Some gentle movement work can help to encourage supple joints and correct posture.

Spider fingers

This game encourages finger dexterity and independence. Put your fingers on the desk and start by trying to make an even sound as each finger rises and drums down on the desk. Make sure that all fingers rise the same distance. Next, put your fingers together as if you have a spider on a mirror. Try to lift each pair of fingers and bring them back together making sure that they meet whilst the other fingers remain firmly together. Try to speed up and see how fast you can go!

Another variation is for the teacher to call the number of the finger to be lifted. This is good for piano pupils as it encourages them to read fingering instructions more easily.

Diaphragm work

This is aimed at wind players although it is useful for all musicians as this exercise reduces tension, allowing the body to move and respond more freely. It should also be noted that there are probably hundreds of useful breathing games – this is just one of my favourites, and is great fun!

Snakes

Take in a deep breath and try to expel it all at speed with a powerful hiss – you should feel tummy muscles working hard! Now put some paper balls on top of the piano or a surface with a height similar to that of your pupils. The pupils should try to hiss them off the piano, racing to see who can do it first – answer, the one who is using their diaphragm the most effectively. This one is hard!

I have suggested a few games, of which there are many variations. You may find that you discover countless versions of your own. As long as you are confident with your approach you will undoubtedly find that the result is improvement in musical performance. So good luck and have fun!

This chapter formed the basis of an article in 'Music Teacher' January 2006.

14

Dealing with Parents

Parents are wonderful – they are the support behind your pupil learning his or her instrument. However, they can be a law unto themselves – I have both encountered their strange ways and experienced it, as a mother. We strive to 'help' our children be successful in life, sometimes pushing too hard and sometimes not hard enough.

The trouble starts for us as teachers when we are dealing with parents who do not understand the demands of learning an instrument. They may not have experienced music in this way before and may have unrealistic expectations. We need to make clear what we are expecting of their child. Neither the pushy parent demanding a grade a year, or the over-relaxed couple who don't support any practice time are much help.

First impressions

When you meet parents for the first time, remember that first impressions are huge – keep relaxed, calm and firm about your requirements as a teacher. Be clear about fees, how and when to pay, how much notice is required for cancellations etc., but also about how much practice is expected and what you hope their child will gain from their lessons.

Parents in the lessons

Sometimes parents may want to sit in to the lesson. With younger children it can be beneficial having someone else involved in the lesson who can help and support the child's practice time with a full understanding of what they are trying to achieve. Even with older children I would always agree to at least one sitting-in session as it shows the parents what to expect and will give them confidence in you. However, as they get older I feel that for a child to learn freely they need to feel independent from their parents and I would suggest that the parent sits outside. The age at which you suggest this is really dependant on the child – there may be some very babyish ten year olds who need parental support, and some very grown up eight year olds who need some independence. Whatever your feeling about this is, you must be firm with what you want the parents to do.

Parental updates

Try to encourage parents to chat about their child's progress whenever you can. If they feel involved they will be much more supportive and they will be pleased to hear how their offspring is getting on.

However this is not always possible and often teachers get little or no contact with parents, especially in state schools where lessons are organised through the local music service. In this instance try to make sure that the school music teacher is updated regularly to ensure that when a parent does want information it is readily available.

Contacing parents

Contacting parents can be a difficult process. It often means making calls in the evenings when you would rather be relaxing and eating dinner, especially as some (though by no means all!), can be rather difficult!

Broaching difficulties

Sometimes you have to meet or speak to parents for the first time under awkward circumstances. There may be an issue which either you feel you need to speak to them about or else they may contact you. They may want to know for example, why their daughter isn't able to take Grade 3 with the rest of her group.

It is easy to get defensive when approached in this way. Instrumental teachers often feel hugely responsible for their pupil's progress. The important thing is to remain calm and professional. Remember that you cannot be responsible for every single aspect of a child's development. Your job is to encourage your pupils in the right direction and hope that they do the rest through their practice.

Ask the parents lots of questions about their feelings and concerns. If a parent feels that you are listening to them and taking on board their viewpoint then not only will you diffuse any frustration or anger they have, but also you will gain their trust. Thank them for speaking to you. Tell them that you appreciate having the conversation. Whatever the problem may be if you can get the parents on side your job will be a million times easier.

You must then gently but firmly explain your viewpoint with confidence and conviction. Remember that you are the specialist in your field and they must understand and respect that for a healthy and successful relationship.

Pushy parents

There are those parents who we encounter who want their little angels to do a grade a year etc. This was discussed in chapter 10. Pushy parents can be calling you at all hours for many things, from trying to establish what needs to be practiced (even though it may be clearly noted in their notebooks), to getting your approval for entering competitions and festivals.

You must be firm with these parents. There will be times when you want and need to switch off and you should make your available contact times clear. For example, if someone rings you after a set time, gently suggest that you are busy now and can talk to them the following day. Otherwise you are in danger of never enjoying your dinner in peace (I speak from experience!).

As far as entering competitions and festivals, you should put a clause in your contract which states the necessity of gaining your approval before entering (see chapter 17 for further details of contracts). When a pupil is on a public platform so is your reputation as a teacher. If they play badly it does not reflect well on you and it will be assumed that you approved them entering even if you haven't. This is not to mention the damaging effect on the pupil's confidence.

Parents must respect your professional opinion and if you are firm they will soon see that you are someone who can be trusted to do the best for their child, in your own way.

15

Dealing with Isolation

Instrumental teachers are often extremely isolated in their work and sometimes don't even see the school music teacher for weeks on end. The need to get between schools quickly leaves little time to get to know other members of staff (or eat lunch!) and the staff room is often an unknown quantity.

In several schools I have wondered what the Head of Music or Music Co-ordinator looks like. He or she may have initially met me and shown me my teaching room / hall / cupboard, where I have been left never to be seen again by this teacher. However, this is not always the case, and in other schools some effort is always made to keep in touch, even if it is only a head around the door every once in a while. Just the most simple communication can make a huge difference, ensuring that the visiting teacher feels valued and that their work is appreciated.

However, even in best music departments it is easy to feel lonely. There are ways to get around this isolation but you will probably need to take the initiative.

• Make time for a coffee break – and venture into the staff room to drink it!

• Get involved in school concerts, whether you are accompanying, playing or even just watching and supporting, teachers, parents and pupils will all be glad of your support.

• Try organising workshops where pupils can practice exam pieces or just enjoy listening to each other play while benefiting from the experience.

• Get permission to take pupils from secondary schools into junior schools, perhaps with some chamber music or a small composing project. This type of activity also acts as a successful recruiting workshop, so is good for the summer months.

• Track down your point of contact, whether it be the Head of Music or another teacher or admin member, every few weeks. You may have concerns over non-attendance or want to put forward a student for a concert. Any excuse may do to remind them that you are present and doing a good job!

The problem is that generally teachers are not paid for many extracurricular events (or even a coffee break!). It is therefore up to you to decide how much to try to become involved. Remember that in the long run giving up some of your time can lead to your skills being more in demand, therefore increased hours and consequently increased pay. You may also find yourself in a position where you can choose which work you would like to accept and what to turn down. You will feel more comfortable in your work environment, and consequently in your teaching and it is your pupils who will feel the benefit.

16

Other Teachers

One of the problems, which may occur in your teaching career, is encountering other teachers, either before, during or after your time with a particular student.

Following a teacher – especially a much-loved teacher – is generally difficult only if you don't feel comfortable with their teaching methods. Perhaps you feel that they have let a pupil get into technical problems. As a professional you will not want to 'bad mouth' your predecessor, yet correcting problems can be a long and difficult task, and a full explanation of why you need to tackle this problem when a previous teacher did not may be awkward.

At one high school I taught at, I consistently had flute and clarinet pupils who had come from a woodwind teacher whose primary instrument was the flute. Her flute teaching was second to none and each child came to me with a sound technique and confident tone, usually with a couple of successful exam results under their belts to boot. However, with the clarinettists it was another issue.

The problem was primarily a lack of understanding of embouchure and how to improve it. Children can often make a reasonable sound on the clarinet with any old embouchure in the early days. It is a satisfying sound, the pupils feel that they are making quick progress and can soon be playing tunes well, despite tell-tale signs that their badly shaped embouchure will soon lead them into problems.

I was then faced with pupils who thought they were doing really well and couldn't understand why, when faced with more difficult music or some light tonguing passages, they were struggling. Trying to change a child's embouchure because they have hit a brick wall is demoralising for both the child and teacher and can even result in pupils giving up. It is vital that the child still feels that they are making progress, which is exceptionally difficult when they feel that they have gone backwards not forwards!

Explaining all this to parents is hard without saying that they were badly taught in the first place (especially when it is highly likely that younger brothers and sisters may be still having lessons with the other teacher). You must preserve your own reputation and simply try to explain the problem as delicately as you can.

Not the only teacher?
Occasionally you may find that you are not the only teacher on the scene. Well-meaning parents sometimes think that they are doing the best thing by getting their child a teacher both at home and at school. Usually the teacher who came along first will retain the status of being the main teacher whilst the other teacher may take on a supplementary role.

You may be lucky and find that your technique and teaching styles are complementary. However, problems arise when there are differences of approach or you clash with another more competitive teacher.

The best solution is always to contact the other teacher. In one case I had a flute pupil who I had taught before I went on maternity leave. She didn't get on with the covering teacher and consequently her parents found her a teacher out of school. When I returned she wanted to have lessons with me once again but she didn't want to stop lessons with her new teacher who she liked immensely and who had entered her for her Grade 5 exam.

As it turned out, the other teacher was someone who I had met a few times and also got on well with. We agreed that she would cover all the technical aspects of the pieces, and I would accompany the pupil as well as prepare her for the aural, scales and sight-reading. The pupil claimed that she never felt confused – something that we were both concerned not to do – and she benefited from our differing experiences. The partnership worked exceptionally well and the pupil got a distinction!

On another occasion I discovered that a beginner saxophonist, who I taught for a short fifteen minute lesson each week, was having extra lessons with another of my pupils. The teacher–pupil was someone who I had taught for many years and although she was primarily a clarinettist and not a saxophonist she was charging the other girl for an hour lesson and hugely undercutting my own fees.

I was obviously concerned for two reasons. The first and primary reason was that I was sceptical about the older girl's teaching abilities, due to her limited experience. Secondly, I was somewhat put out that she thought she could 'undercut' my professional experience!

The parents of the younger girl did contact me to talk it over and were quite adamant that they wanted the extra lessons to be supporting my role as the primary teacher. The result was that I ended up with a 'helper' who supported my teaching as discussed and directed by me. For example, I was able to ask for the older girl to help with tonguing and slurring in a particular piece, which meant in my lesson I could concentrate on expression and playing creatively. As a bonus my older pupil learnt some (I hope) sound teaching techniques, which in turn helped her own playing!

17

Teaching Conditions

In an age where people start suing as soon as they sneeze, it is important that as teachers we ensure our backs are covered.

Contract

This section is relevant mainly to self-employed teachers, as county teachers are generally well looked after and should find themselves with a decent contract as a matter of course.

If you are self-employed make sure that your contract is watertight. We are in a vulnerable position as instrumental teachers – parents don't understand that we are not employed by the school, and as schools often declare themselves devoid of any responsibility for your teaching there, you can face a nightmare when things go wrong.

There are two types of contract which you should hold – the first is with the school, even if you are there on a completely self-employed basis with no money changing hands whatsoever, you should have some form of contract which lays down your teaching conditions. For example, you should include a clause to say that there should be adequate teaching space with a piano (if required) in a room with a window in the door (legal requirement for one-on-one teaching). Also you need to know what support they will give you in the event of having to contact parents to recover unpaid fees or because a child stops lessons without notice. Finally, you need to know the terms under which you would be required to stop teaching at the school and what the notice period would be (this protects you against unfair dismissal).

Your second contract is even more important as this is with the parents. This contract is vital as you often don't have much contact with the parents. Your income is at risk without it as you should require that the parent or carer who signs the contract is required to give a notice period e.g. half a term. You can also set out what you expect from pupils and parents regarding practice and your policy on exams and competitions.

Sometimes schools may have set contracts for visiting teachers to send to parents. Read it carefully – you are the one signing it and not the school! For further advice on how to draft appropriate contracts and up to date information look at the ISM or MU websites and see the section below.

Finance

If you are self-employed one of the biggest headaches is dealing with finance. If you are partly employed and partly self-employed then this headache gets bigger!

The best advice is to find an accountant who understands the business that you are in. There are many things that you can claim for which are not always recognised – for example, instrumental tuition for yourself. Lists are published by both the MU and ISM, which detail these items. If you are in a union seek their help and advice – you will find that unions may offer a reduced rate to members for accountancy services.

Keep careful records of whom you teach and what you charge for group and individuals. Don't be tempted to take on cash-only pupils – so many teachers have fallen down when the tax office have decided to randomly investigate people. The school will confirm who is having lessons, so you may be found out and at worse case could lose your work at that school as well as face heavy fines.

Teaching space

The space in which we teach is often confined to tiny rooms, cupboards, staff rooms etc., which are often not hugely appropriate. It is rarely possible to change this however, it is important to try and improve what space is available. For example, if you find yourself in a classroom don't be afraid to create a useful working space by moving unwanted furniture, instruments or clutter. Working in a corner of a room which has desks and chairs set up for a class lesson, gives a sense of being somewhere you don't belong. It lessens the importance of what you are doing. We must not let our pupils feel that we are not engaging in a worthwhile activity; so make time to make the space more effective. Set up your stands so that you and your pupil can move freely and can see each other easily and comfortably. To not make this effort suggests a sloppier approach to the lessons, less focus on the work involved and consequent loss of importance put on practice time – eventually slower progress!

Sticking to regulations

There are certain regulations that relate to one-on-one teaching which you should make yourself aware of. For example, legally you should have a window in the door of your teaching room. If this is not the case then you must always teach with the door partially open. Points such as this one are important in protecting ourselves from false accusations. In one instance a male teacher lost his job because a female student accused him of indecent assault, however in court she later admitted that it was a false accusation to get attention from her warring parents.

For a full list of up to date teaching regulations you should contact the MU or ISM and any breach of these regulations should be first addressed to the school. If nothing is done, then you should inform your union, who may well take up the case to ensure that you are working in a proper environment.

Physical contact

Many teachers deem it is necessary to use physical contact to correct things such as posture or hand position. However, you are not legally allowed to do this and put yourself at risk if you do so.

If you feel you really cannot teach without some physical contact then you should either obtain written permission or get another adult present for that lesson. You may need to set boundaries in your contract or develop a policy document about what you will need to do and what will be avoided. However, it is far preferable to develop other solutions such as using a mirror or another student to demonstrate your points.

If a situation should occur you should say nothing to the people present but contact your union immediately.

Systems of retrieving missing pupils

Most schools have a pupil receptionist or 'runner' who can find your missing pupil for you. Music departments usually have a telephone so that you can call reception to organise this and most receptionists are quite amenable to looking up timetables and locating pupils.

However, sometimes the runner isn't always available or is on another mission. The receptionist may be busy or unhappy about looking up missing pupils and even when you discover where the child is you may then have to locate a room on the opposite side of the school, which could well be on Mars for all you know about how to get there! By the time you have the child on his or her way to you and you are safely back in your teaching room, you may well find that the lesson time has ended and the next pupil is knocking on the door.

My advice on this is to send for pupils where possible but devise other ways of helping them to remember their lesson times. A system of missed lesson slips which can be put into class registers (ask reception where they are – they may well do this for you), or sent to the pupil via the runner seems to work well. If a pupil misses several lessons in a row without explanation, then the Head of Music should be made aware of the situation.

If you are self-employed and paid directly by the parents, I would strongly advise parent contact at this stage too. My own system is to send the missing pupil slip home on the third missed lesson (although I send for them within school as soon as they are late). Parents like to know what's going on and will be on your side as long as you keep them informed. A note of the next lesson will help them to remind the pupil when they should attend.

NB. In primary schools there is rarely a need to chase pupils as classroom teachers are often more aware of the timetable than the instrumental teacher! It is more often the case that pupils are there waiting and all set up ahead of you! However, if you do have someone who has forgotten it is generally much easier to find pupils as the schools are so much smaller.

Pupil non-attendance

There may be many reasons why pupils in schools do not attend their lessons, and whilst I have found that they are always in a minority, some schools are more prone to this than others. For example, in one private school I have had only three cases of continual non-attendance in seven years, yet in some state schools this is much higher.

Of the three private school girls, one girl had simply lost interest and no amount of redirection, duets, jazz or pop tunes could rekindle it.

Another suffered from continual illness and on talking to her parents we discovered that she simply didn't have the energy to practise but was scared to admit it. Some gentle revision over a few weeks and reassurance that she only had to practice when she felt well meant that she was able to continue and a year later she achieved Grade 3 with merit.

The third one just couldn't cope with the change from junior to senior school. In this school pupils move up to the senior school in year 6, a whole year earlier than state schools, coping with timetables and room changes is in itself a major task at that age. Coming to a clarinet lesson meant checking a rotating timetable, and remembering to leave the correct lesson just proved too much. Again it was through contact with her parents that we resolved the matter, and with a little help from her friends she finally got into a routine.

In each case there was no problem that could not be resolved. Lessons continued successfully with the second two and the first girl was able to focus on other activities.

Of course in some cases the parents are not much help. One girl's non-attendance at a state school was brought to the attention of the parents by means of a note sent home. I had no response and kept trying to summon the girl in school but to no avail. It was only when the next term's bills were due that it seemed that both parent and child were in hiding!

Unions

Instrumental teachers across the UK are members of various unions from the NUT to the Musicians' Union. The most relevant to the instrumental teaching profession are the MU (Musicians' Union), and the ISM (Incorporated Society of Musicians).

ISM

The ISM state three prime objectives: to represent and protect the interests of everyone who works with music; to raise practical and ethical standards within the profession; and to provide members with the best quality advice and benefits. Benefits include £10 million public liability insurance and legal expenses in the EU, a very successful legal advice service, a 24-hour legal and tax help line. Tax investigation insurance

Further Information

www.tda.gov.uk or
www.canteach.gov.uk for various
relevant documents from child
protection issues, to dealing with
violent pupils.

GTC's (General Teaching Council)
Code of Professional Values and
Practice for Teachers

www.musicians.org.uk or email:
teachers@musiciansunion.org.uk

www.ism.org

and tax return service, legal representation, counselling helpline and many others. There are also various events and workshops taking place around the country.

MU

The MU maintains an active role in music education and promises to lobby and campaign on all issues faced by its members. It has an in-house solicitor who can offer free legal advice to MU members. They are currently establishing a national teachers' section to help to facilitate this and they currently produce various fact-sheets and guidance notes on all aspects of instrumental teaching such as teaching rates. You can apply for a teacher disclosure through SOUND SENSE for a standard fee, which can be useful, if you are required to obtain this yourself.

18

Conclusion:
Continuation and Motivation

Why a pupil first decided to learn an instrument is an important fact to consider when trying to understand why they want to give up. For many Grade 5 is a cut off, but why is this the case? How can we as teachers ensure that pupils get the most out of their lessons and are driven to continue and succeed? We must adapt and reinvent teaching techniques, finding way to keep pupils engaged and motivated.

If a child does decide to give up then it is worth trying to get to the root of the problem. The spark that led them to play that particular instrument may still be there and there may be a different reason why they have lost their motivation. A simple case of boredom with pieces or musical styles may be easily rectified with a change of repertoire or by trying something new like some jazz improvisation. It may be that peer pressure is making it 'uncool' or they are missing a sports club to be at the lesson, in which case a change of lesson time may be enough to keep them interested. You may well find that you can offer a resolution and sometimes they will then go on to do great things... I myself announced that I wanted to stop at 15 – only to go on and make it my career.

If the stress of doing exams is creating an environment where they no longer enjoy playing their instrument, then pupils may need to avoid exams. It is important for the teacher to support this. An interest in exams may be rekindled at a later date if necessary, but what is more important is that the pupil can continue to learn for enjoyment.

The wrong mix of teaching group can also create a problem, especially if one child is stronger than another. If this happens but there is no alternative group then give two shorter individual lessons (it may not be possible if there are three in the group!). You will need to get them organised so that they have instruments at the ready before the lesson and don't waste time setting up in the lesson – but 10 minutes quality one-on-one time can work wonders for a child who feels that they are being left behind. A few weeks like this may be all you need to rekindle their enjoyment of the instrument.

One of the reasons that make pupils give up is that they don't like their teacher. This is something that all teachers need to embrace at some point in their career. No one can be all things to all people and whilst it is important to try to reach pupils in whatever manner you can, if in the long run you are ending up teaching in a way which doesn't suit you perhaps this is the time to suggest changing teacher. With careful discussion you may be able to help the child find a more suitable teacher. The important thing is not to take it to heart. You are only going to make yourself stressed and unhappy when you should be concentrating on doing the best thing for that pupil and then moving on to concentrate on your remaining pupils.

It is also important to recognise that children's interests change as they grow up. If they have simply outgrown their desire to play an instrument then it is better to allow them to give up than to see them continue because parents believe they should. They will only end up resenting you and the lesson time and are unlikely to make any progress, which will compound the problem. Instead perhaps in the future they will once again pick up their instrument and as an adult be able to remember and rekindle the fun they had whilst they were learning at school.

Further Reading

A Common Approach: A Framework for an Instrumental/Vocal Curriculum (2002) England, Federation of Music Services / National Association of Music Educators, London: Faber.

Instrumental Teaching and Learning in Context: Sharing a Curriculum for Music Education (1995) England, Music Advisers' National Association, now NAME.

Benson, Jarlath (1987), **Working more Creatively with Groups**, London: Tavistock.

Harris, P and Crozier, R (2000) **The Music Teacher's Companion: A Practical Guide**, London: ABRSM Publishing.

Ditchfield, Diana **'Dyslexia and Music'** - in Dyslexia - Successful Inclusion in the Secondary School. Eds. Lindsay Peer and Gavin Reid (2001). Published in Association with the British Dyslexia Association.

Hallam, Susan (1998), **Instrumental Teaching: A Practical Guide to Better Teaching and Learning**, Oxford: Heinnemann.

Ed. Harris P and Crozier R (2000) **The Music Teacher's Companion,** London: ABRSM Publishing.

Harris, P (1994) **Improve Your Sight-Reading!**, London: Faber Music.

Harris, P (2000) **Perfect Your Sight-Reading!**, London: Faber Music.

Lovelock , William (1965) **Common Sense in Music Teaching**, London: G.E Bell.

Ed. Marks, (2004) **All Together! Teaching Music in Groups**, London ABRSM: Publishing.

Miles, T R and Westcombe, J (2001) **Music and Dyslexia: Opening New Doors**, London: Whurr Publishers.

Mills, J (2005), **Music in the School**, Oxford: Oxford University Press.

Odam, G (1995), **The Sounding Symbol: Music Education in Action**, Cheltenham: Stanley Holmes.

Oglethorpe, S (1996), **Instrumental Music for**

Dyslexics: a Teaching Handbook, London: Whurr Publishers.

Ed. Peer, L and Reid, G (2001), **Dyslexia – Successful Inclusion in the Secondary School London**, David Fulton Publishers.

Sloboda, J (1985), **The Musical Mind: The Cognitive Psychology of Music**. Oxford: Clarendon Press.

Ed. Spruce, G (1996), **Teaching Music,** London: Routledge/Open University.

Ed. Stringer, M (2005), **The Music Teacher's Handbook**, London: Faber.

Swanick, K (1988), **Music Mind and Education**, London: Routledge.

Swanick, K (1994) **Musical Knowledge: Intuition, Analysis and Music Education**, London: Routledge.

Swanick, K (1999) **Teaching Music Musically**, London: Routledge.

Useful Websites

Qualifications

www.tda.gov.uk or
www.canteach.gov.uk
for further information about
teaching in the UK.

www.teachinginscotland.com for
information about teaching
in Scotland.

www.openuniversity.co.uk for
information about the OU's flexible
PGCE which many instrumental
teachers have found useful.

Unions

Musicians' Union,
www.musicians.org.uk
or email: teachers@
musiciansunion.org.uk

International Society of
Musicians, www.ism.org

Teaching Societies

British Kodaly Institute,
www.britishkodalyac.demon.co.uk

British Suzuki Institute, email:
bsi@suzukimusic.force9.co.uk

Special Needs

Melody provides help, support
and ideas for teachers, parents
and carers, www.melody.me.uk

The British Dyslexia Association
www.bda-dyslexia.org.uk
or email
info@dyslexiahelp-bda.
demon.uk

National Music and Disability
Information, email
info@soundsense.org

National Down Syndrome
Society, www.ndss.org or
Down Syndrome Educational
Trust, www.downsed.org

National Autistic Society,
www.nas.org

British Institute of Learning
Disabilities, www.bild.org.uk